W9-BOF-748

Book Design by Paul Ferrini
and Lisa Carta

Library of Congress Control Number
2007927640

ISBN # 978-1-879159-70-9

Heartways Press
9 Phillips Street, Greenfield MA 01301
www.heartwayspress.com

Manufactured in the United States of America

Discovering the Radiant Light Within

Paul Ferrini

Opening Blessing

May these words

awaken the radiant light

and boundless love

that lie within you

Table of Contents

Introduction

The Hidden Jewel is so small we cannot see it. And it is so big we cannot imagine it. Infinitely great and small, it is beyond name and form.

That is why it is so difficult to locate or describe. At best, we can point to it or catch a glimpse of it as it moves in and out, up and down, around us and through us.

We say it rests in the heart, yet there is no place where it cannot be found.

Each Self inheres in the All and the All inheres in the Self. That is the mystery. To know the Self, is to know the All.

The body of this work is long and deep. I have rolled it up into a nutshell. If you crack the shell open, you will see all of it at a glance.

Then, you will know where you stand.

Lao Tzu told us that Tao is the mother of the myriad things. Our Core Self is cradled in the arms of this Mother. As she rocks back and forth, she falls asleep. When she wakes up, we are shaken from her womb. We emerge naked and afraid. We cry out. It is the beginning of the journey.

In the end, we will return to the Great Womb of the Mother. For now, we have work to do. We must move through the dream with its trespasses and hurts. We must learn to forgive ourselves and others.

Hansel and Gretel cast scraps of bread along the path through the forest so that they could find their way home. But the birds ate them.

Those birds know something we don't. But they cannot tell us. We have to take the journey into the woods. We have to feel our way home along the dark path.

We need not be afraid. Our destination is as certain as the path we travel. Regardless of how often the path twists and turns, it will guide us back home.

All who begin the journey will complete it. It is only a matter of time.

If we are patient, we will enjoy the journey. We will hear the rushing waters as we walk beside the stream. We will rest upon the rocks and breathe in the scent of pine and cedar. We will hear the song of the woodthrush and see the dance of the red tailed hawks circling overhead.

May we travel happily along the path. In this moment and in all moments to come, may we remember how deeply and profoundly we are guided and blessed.

Namaste,

Paul Ferrini

The Hidden Jewel

1

Our happiness is directly proportionate
to our ability to see and experience
our innocence and that of others.

2

To see our innocence is to know
that we are worthy of love.

3

Our worthiness does not derive
from anything that we say or do.
It comes with our beingness.
It is therefore unconditional,
everpresent and eternal.

4

When we know in our hearts and minds
the innocence and essential worth of all beings,
We live in harmony and in peace.
We experience the ecstatic nature
of love without conditions.

5

The Core Self is Innocent.
It cannot be wounded nor can it attack others.
It wishes only to love and be loved.
This eternal one lives inside each one of us.
It is our very essence.

6

The Core Self is the hidden jewel within.
It is who we are at the most fundamental level.
It includes in their potential
all the gifts and talents we possess.
It is what makes us unique.
It is the blueprint we are born with.

7

All of us have a Core Self,
but not many of us are in touch with it.
That is because the Core Self can be encountered
only with unconditional love and acceptance

8

When we are connected to our Core Self,
we are connected to all that is.
We live in relationship to our Source
We abide in who we are.

9

The Core Self is not in the world.
It is in our heart of hearts.
The True Self is the expression
of the Core Self in the world.
It is in the world, but not of the world.

10

All of the talents and gifts of Our Core Self
are developed and expressed by our True Self.

11

The True Self is the engine of our creative expression.
Because it is aligned with the Core Self,
the True Self is energy incarnate.
It harnesses the kundalini energy
and puts it to work in our lives.

12

The Core Self is a noun, an essence, a potential.
The True Self is a verb.
It is action, movement, fulfillment.

13

The Core Self is about Being.
The True Self is about Doing.

14

Doing must always be in alignment with Being
or it will be wrong-doing.
All the work of the False Self is wrong-doing.
It is action without heart.
It is all about trespass and betrayal.

15

When Doing comes into alignment with Being,
action is heartfelt. It honors self and others.
This leads to right doing, right livelihood,
and right relationship.

16

When the True Self asserts itself,
we are reborn in integrity.
We become authentic and naturally
align with our Spiritual Purpose.
We live not from the outside in,
but from the inside out.
Our life is no longer driven by fear
and run by our ego.
It is inspired by love and
directed by the indwelling Spirit.

The False Self

17

The False Self arises with the experience
of separateness and inequality.
All trespasses have their origin here.

18

We call it the False Self
because it is an illusion.
It is not ultimately real.
Only the Core Self is real.

19

The False Self establishes
and lives in a world
where people hurt each other
and live in a vicious cycle
of betrayal and abuse.

20

In the world of the False Self
all of us trespass,
all of us are wounded,
and every one of us
harbors guilt and resentment.

21

If we did not harbor guilt and resentment,
we would not live in this world.
We live here because we need to learn
to heal and to forgive.

22

This world is the place we create
and the place where we go
when we cease to be aware
of The Core Self
in ourselves and others.

23

Without our connection
to our Core Self
and the awareness
that we are worthy of love,
we cannot create anything helpful
to ourselves or to others.

24

In order to create wisely,
We must know what we really want.
That means our False Self has to shatter first.
Because what the False Self wants
is not what we really want.
It is what others want for us
or what we think they want.

25

The False Self seeks to please
or appease others.
It cannot create for our highest good
or the highest good of others.
That can be done only through
the connection to the Core Self.

26

Because the False Self does not create
in alignment with the Core Self,
it cannot create harmony.
It cannot create right relationship
or right livelihood.

27

The action of the False Self
is not in alignment with our Essence or our Source.
When doing and Being are not in alignment
wrong-doing results.

28

Because it creates out of its woundedness,
the False Self creates only pain and suffering.
It cannot escape from the cycle
of its own violent thoughts,
feelings and actions.

29

Yet this world of the False Self
with all its fearful creations
is false and illusory.
It is not the truth about us.

30

When we know this without any doubt,
we wake up. We stop suffering.
We no longer participate in the dream.
We no longer react to the drama.
We see only the Core Self
in ourselves and others.

31

The Core Self lives in Heaven.
The False Self lives in Hell.
The Self we align with determines
the world in which we live.

Forgiving Ourselves

32

Waking up is difficult
only because we do not see
the truth about ourselves
or because we don't believe
the truth we see.

33

To see the truth we must stop looking
through the eyes of the False Self
and learn to see with our hearts.

34

To meet the Core Self
we must heal all perceived wounds
as well as the resentment and guilt
associated with them.

35

This seems easy enough until we realize
that we are attached to our wounds
and to our stories about them.

36

It is not easy for us to let go
of the drama of shame and blame.
It is not easy for us to forgive each other
and thus put an end to
our guilt and our grievances.

37

For most of us, waking up
means not just changing our minds,
but also healing our hearts.
It requires forgiveness not just of others,
but also of ourselves.

38

In order to forgive others,
we must learn to forgive ourselves.
We must take ourselves off the cross.
Then we can release others.

39

Forgiving ourselves is our greatest challenge.
Learning to be gentle and compassionate with ourselves
is our most important spiritual practice.

40

All of us have come into this world
to learn one lesson.
We have come here to learn
how to love ourselves without conditions.

41

It is true that other people judge us
and/or try to control us
and we need to learn to forgive them
for their trespasses against us.
It is also true that we judge
and try to control others
and we need to ask for their forgiveness
and learn to forgive ourselves
for our trespasses against them.
But all this is preliminary work.
It just prepares us for the real work
we have come here to do.

42

Your real work is to find
the person who has betrayed you
and whom you cannot forgive.
When you know who that person is
you begin to wake up.
That person is you.

43

Behind all judgment and condemnation of others
is self judgment and self condemnation.
Behind all judgment and condemnation of self
is shame and unworthiness.
That is where we find the core wound
that needs to be healed.

44

When we heal our core wound,
we remove the shroud that stands between us
and our core self.

45

That is when we wake up.
That is when we are reborn in Spirit.
That is when the False Self falls away
and the True Self is born.

Taking off Our Mask

46

The False Self believes that it is unworthy,
insufficient, damaged and unlovable
and/or it believes that others are.
It feels less than or better than,
inferior or superior to others.
In addressing self or other, it uses
the language of shame and blame.

47

Because it has been hurt,
the False Self believes that it is bad
or that someone else is.
Shame becomes its condition
and blame of self or other
its modus operandi.

48

When the False Self arises,
our innocence is lost or shrouded
so that it cannot be seen.

49

This is known as our fall from Grace.
We are disconnected from our Core Self,
from the Core Self of others
and from our Source.

50

This disconnection is psychologically painful.
Even though it is ultimately false or unreal,
it feels real enough. It hurts.

51

Now we have a choice.
We can feel that pain or we can try to escape it.

52

As a diversion, we can seek pleasure.
We can become addicted
to drugs, alcohol, sex, food or work.
That builds a chemical wall around our pain
so that we no longer see it or feel it.

53

To avoid facing our pain
we can go into denial
and pretend the pain does not exist.
We can build a mask and pretend to be happy.
That is what most of us do.
We cover up our pain and seal it with a smiley face.

54

We don't want others to see our pain
because we think that they would reject us
if they knew how we really felt about ourselves.
The depth of our shame is so great
we often would rather die
than let others see our pain.

55

The False Self has two components:
a shadow and a mask.
The shadow contains the pain,
the fear, the shame and unworthiness
that we don't want others to see.
The mask is the disguise
that hides them from sight.

56

Behind the mask
within the dark terrain of the shadow
lies the trauma of our wound.
This powerful repressed energy
runs our life unconsciously,
jerking us around
like a marionette on a string.

57

As long as it remains unseen and unacknowledged,
our core wound will be unconsciously triggered,
creating emotional upheaval and distress
in our relationship with others.

58

There are two masks that must be taken off
if we wish to encounter our Core Self.

59

First we must remove the mask
that disguises our pain.
We must stop pretending to be happy
when we are not.
We must acknowledge our pain
and begin to bring love
to the wounded parts of ourselves.

60

When the first mask is removed,
the shadow is integrated.
We learn to accept all of ourselves.
The psychological division
between dark and light,
persona and shadow
is bridged and the psyche
returns to wholeness.

61

The more we learn to bring
love and acceptance,
the more our core wound
begins to heal
and the unworthiness
and shame attached to it
begin to fall away.

62

Now the second mask is peeled back
and we begin to see our innocence.

63

For the wound, being unreal,
is also a cloak or a disguise.
When the wound heals,
the cloak is removed
and our Core Self is revealed
in all its magnificence.

The Birth of the True Self

64

All this is a natural result
of our healing journey.
We cannot rush it or fake it.
It happens because we keep showing up,
even when the path is steep and hard,
because we continue to hold our fears
and those of others
gently and with compassion.

65

The birth of the True Self
is often called a Spiritual Awakening experience.
It is not always a pleasant experience,
because the old self that betrayed us must die
for the new self that honors us to be born.

66

It takes great courage to go willingly
into the dark depths of our psyche
to reclaim the light.
Many spiritual students try to skip
this part of the journey.
They try to manifest their dreams
before they have touched their pain.
Of course, it doesn't work.
Real happiness is not possible
without deep emotional healing.

67

If we want to build a house,
we have to build the foundation first.
Then we can put up the walls and the roof.
If we want to manifest our dreams,
we have to heal our wounds
and recover our innocence.
Then we can meet the Core Self
and learn to be true to it.

68

The death of the False Self
is often neither quick nor easy.
We simultaneously try
to surrender and keep control.
We do a strange, contorted dance
that often ends in total exhaustion.
Until then our ego refuses
to admit defeat.

69

In the end we realize that we are not the doer,
but the one through whom it is done.
We get out of the way and let Spirit
move us how and where it wills.

70

Once we surrender to Spirit
and begin to honor our Core Self
we can no longer betray it.
We have no choice but to become
completely honest and authentic.

71

Once the True Self rises up in us
we can no longer be false to anyone.
We see and greet the authentic self
in every person we meet.

72

The phoenix rises from the ashes
of the purifying fire.
From the death of the ego,
the True Self rises
in its shining purity and strength.

73

When the Truth Self is born
our lives change, sometimes drastically.
We can no longer live in sacrifice or self-betrayal.
The nature of our work and our relationships change.
Work becomes service to the divine.
Relationship becomes sacred union.

74

Our old life comes to an end
and a new life begins.
Like the butterfly we emerge from the chrysalis
with brightly colored wings.
Our ego-driven, worldly life is over.
Our Spirit-directed life
of surrender and service begins.

75

Now we recognize our gifts,
learn to trust them and offer them
without strings attached.
A new creative energy moves through us,
guiding and sustaining us,
inspiring and uplifting others.
Our spiritual purpose
becomes increasingly clear
and we are happily drawn to fulfill it.

76

This is not the end of our journey
but a new beginning.
Now that we have come home
we invite others to join us.
Bread and wine are set out
upon the table.
All who are hungry and thirsty
are invited to eat and to drink.

77

Now the opposites are touching.
Yin and Yang, high and low,
great and small, are entwined
and embracing each other.
Alpha and omega are joined
in one unbroken circle
of love and atonement.

78

Rejoice and give thanks
for Christ is born within us.
The Buddha nature has awakened
and the sins of all sentient beings
have been forgiven.

79

The Spirit of God has descended
and lives and moves among us.
It rises and falls with our breath
and blows gently over the waters.

80

The seed has sprouted
and the plant has bloomed.
You can see the flowers
and smell their fragrance.
The promise made long ago
has now been fulfilled.

81

Human and the divine are now one.
Heaven has come to earth and earth has risen
with all its daughters and sons.
Not one of them has been found unworthy.
Not a single one has been rejected or left behind.
All have been redeemed and blessed.
All have safely returned home.

Closing Blessing

May the words you have read
awaken the True Self within you.
May they inspire you
to give and receive
love without conditions.
May they open your heart
to ecstasy and bliss.
Namaste.

Paul Ferrini is the author of over 30 books on love, healing and forgiveness. His unique blend of spirituality and psychology goes beyond self-help and recovery into the heart of healing. His conferences, retreats, and *Affinity Group Process* have helped thousands of people deepen their practice of forgiveness and open their hearts to the divine presence in themselves and others.

For more information on Paul's work, visit the web-site at ***www.paulferrini.com.*** The website has many excerpts from Paul Ferrini's books, as well as information on his workshops and retreats. Be sure to request Paul's free email newsletter, as well as a free catalog of his books and audio products. You can also email: info@**heartwayspress.com** or write to **Heartways Press, 9 Phillips Steet, Greenfield, MA 01301.**

Explore the Other Spiritual Mastery Books

If you like this book, you may want to read the other books in the series. They are briefly described below.

The first book— *The Laws of Love*—contains ten essential spiritual principles that we need to master in order to heal and step into our life purpose.

The second book— *The Power of Love*—contains ten spiritual practices that help us connect with our Core Self, our Source, and the gift that we are here to give.

The third book— *The Presence of Love*—helps us understand the masculine/feminine aspects of the Divine and shows us how to embody the unconditional love that will heal us and our planet.

The fourth book—*Love is My Gospel*—looks at the life and teachings of one spiritual master (Jesus) as an example of what is possible for us.

The fifth book —*Real Happiness*—shows us how to heal our wounds at depth and awaken the joy that is our birthright.

The sixth book—*Embracing Our True Self*—describes the three stages in the process of healing and transformation and offers case histories of people who have transformed their lives in our community.

The seventh book— *The Real Happiness Workbook*—offers readers an in-depth experiential process that is necessary for their healing and empowerment.

Paul Ferrini's Course in Spiritual Mastery

Part Seven: Real Happiness—The Workbook

Creating Your Personal Roadmap
to a Joyful and Empowered Life
96 pages $14.95
ISBN # 978-1-879159-71-6

Part Six: Embracing Our True Self

A New Paradigm Approach to Healing Our Wounds,
Finding Our Gifts, and Fulfilling Our Spiritual
Purpose
192 pages $13.95
ISBN # 978-1-879159-69-3

Part Five: Real Happiness

A Roadmap for Healing Our Pain and Awakening
the Joy That Is Our Birthright
160 pages $12.95
ISBN # 978-1-879159-68-6

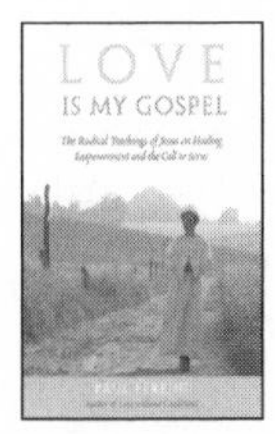

Part Four: Love is My Gospel

The Radical Teachings of Jesus on Healing,
Empowerment and the Call to Serve
128 pages $12.95
ISBN # 1-879159-67-8

Part Three: The Presence of Love

God's Answer to Humanity's Call for Help
160 pages $12.95
ISBN # 1-879159-62-7

Part Two: The Power of Love

10 Spiritual Practices that Can Transform Your Life
168 pages $12.95
ISBN # 1-879159-61-9

Part One: The Laws of Love

A Guide to Living in Harmony
with Universal Spiritual Truth
144 pages $12.95
ISBN # 1-879159-60-0

Paul's In-depth Presentation of the Laws of Love on 9 CDs

THE LAWS OF LOVE

Part One (5 CDs) ISBN # 1-879159-58-9 $49.00
Part Two (4 CDs) ISBN # 1-879159-59-7 $39.00

These are only a few of the many titles available.
To order or receive a free catalog of Paul Ferrini's Books and Audio products, contact: Heartways Press 9 Phillips Street, Greenfield, MA 01301   413-774-9474
Toll free: 1-888-HARTWAYemail: info@heartwayspress.com
You may also purchase these products on our website

www.Paul Ferrini.com

Paul Ferrini's Real Happiness Workshop

By Real Happiness we mean the ability to be true to ourselves, kind to others, and able to weather the ups and downs of life with acceptance and compassion.

This powerful workshop is designed to help us learn to love and accept ourselves radically and profoundly. Participants will learn to:

- Accept, nurture and bring love to themselves.
- Be true to themselves and live honestly and authentically.
- Make and accept responsibility for their own decisions.
- Discover their talents/gifts and find their passion/purpose.
- Cultivate an open heart and an open mind.
- Forgive and learn from their mistakes.
- Be patient with the process of healing and transformation.
- Cultivate a positive attitude toward life and see obstacles as challenges.
- Develop the capacity to hear their inner guidance and surrender to their spiritual purpose.

A genuinely happy person lives in *Right Relationship* to self and others and engages in *Right Livelihood*, expressing his or her gifts and bringing joy to self and others. These are therefore the goals of this work.

This workshop is available in both a one-day and two-day format. For more information about how you can bring this workshop to your community call us at 1-888-HARTWAY.